THE DEFINITIVE COMMUNITY COLLEGE GUIDE

A CONCISE ROADMAP TO ACADEMIC SUCCESS

DANIEL PAGE
M.L.I.S., M.S., B.A.

PublishAmerica
Baltimore

First printing

PublishAmerica has allowed this work to remain exactly as the author intended, verbatim, without editorial input.

ISBN: 1-60474-896-6
PUBLISHED BY PUBLISHAMERICA, LLLP
www.publishamerica.com
Baltimore

Printed in the United States of America

DEDICATION

This book is dedicated to my family for their love and to my colleagues for giving me an opportunity to serve. I am especially grateful to my dear friend Denny Edwards for sharing her expertise during the publication of this book.

PREFACE

Community colleges are increasingly becoming an integral part of the educational landscape of America. In 2007, there were almost twelve million students enrolled in community colleges across the nation, and community colleges could boast of having forty-six percent of the total undergraduate population in the country (AACC Research and Statistics). As the number of students in community colleges increases, and as these institutions play an increasingly important role in America, there will continue to be a great need to help students make the most of their academic career. Over the past decade, I have had the opportunity to experience both the perspective of a student and that of an employee at various community colleges. In this book, I hope to share some of the insights I learned through those experiences. This book presents helpful guidance to assist students in making the most of their time at any perspective community college and is primarily designed for students enrolled in a community college, technical school, or other two-year educational institution. It is intended to be a concise guide that can be read in a shorter amount of time and still give students a solid foundation for success.

First time students, returning students, nontraditional students, and those considering enrolling in a two-year college can all benefit from the resources of this book. The content was chosen because of its importance in making the most of one's time and energy while enrolled in a community college. Questions for reflection are provided at the end of each section, and are designed to enhance the value of the book. Instructors using this book in their classroom presentations are encouraged to solicit their students to complete these questions.

STEP ONE
DREAM BIG

Wherever you are, whoever you are, whenever you read this, always dream big. As you begin to consider how to make the most of your academic career, the first step is to actualize your full potential through dreaming big. Throughout life, your personal aspirations should be set at the highest level. Too many talented individuals never reach their educational, financial, or personal best because they simply do not aspire to reach their highest potential. Often, self-doubt or fear pushes people into a life of mediocrity (or worse). Therefore, to succeed in your educational pursuits, you must first dream big.

DREAM UNIQUELY

Also, the dream that you have for your life needs to be uniquely yours. Sometimes teachers, parents, religious leaders or others try to force people down life paths on which they do not truly belong. As you seek to fulfill your life's best, do not let others force you into a mold that is not truly who or what you are or what you want to become. This does not mean that you should not seek advice from others. Benefiting from the wisdom of others is one of the best resources we have as human beings. At the same time, your dreams need to be uniquely yours, because you have unique talents, desires, and potential. Furthermore, ultimately it is you who has to live with the choices that you make. This is perhaps the best reason to make your dreams uniquely big and uniquely yours.

Your dreams, while big, should also be attainable. Certainly, it is important to push the boundaries of the limits of your dream. Make your dream as large and noble as you can possibly imagine; but, at the same time, your dream should be attainable. For example, I sometimes dream of being the next superhero that will save humanity from its most dangerous threats. This is not a realistic dream, though it is big. I do not plan on jumping from the nearest super structure to my peril in an attempt to defeat my evil nemesis. On the other hand, as a child I could have chosen to make my life's goal to become the first astronaut in my family—a big, but plausible dream. As you contemplate your life's dream, make sure that, with work, time, patience, and energy it is something that can be accomplished in reality.

To develop your dream, think about what you like and what you do not like. As I considered what career I wanted to pursue, I sometimes thought of being a physician. However, I cannot stomach (no pun intended) seeing internal organs, blood, or other fluids that belong to anyone other than myself. For this reason, I marked that big dream off of my list. You should consider what makes you the person that you are, including what you are good at, what you enjoy, and what fulfills your innermost personhood. You then can maximize your future by incorporating your unique talents, pleasures, and interests into your life's attainable dreams.

DREAM BIG, LIVE BIG

One of the greatest destroyers of our goals is living small while dreaming big. Almost anyone can dream up lofty goals for their lives. Fewer are able to make life choices that will lead to the attainment of those dreams. In order to make your dreams a reality, you must map out how you will accomplish your dreams. There is nothing more exciting than to watch your dream become reality as you progress through a series of choices that lead to the fulfillment of your greatest desires. Deciding how to reach your dream will involve making tough decisions. Choosing a career, making family decisions, relocating, and other serious matters must be considered realities in your long term plan. You should write your plan of action down, including specific steps and dates for when you plan to attain each step that will ultimately lead to reaching your goal. Of course, you should expect to make changes to your plan as your progress through the attainment of your life's dream. Sometimes you will advance more quickly or more slowly through certain steps or may decide to alter your plans to progress towards your goals. At the same time, it is vital that you have a specified plan consisting of the decisions and actions you will need to make in order to reach your dream.

Enrolling in a two-year college is one of the most important choices you have made to reach your goals. Fulfilling your dream involves furthering your education and developing your skills. Community colleges provide special environments in which many draw nearer to fulfilling their dreams. The degree programs, certifications, and training that are offered at these institutions provide the necessary preparation for advancing career possibilities and acquiring a greater knowledge and skills base that can greatly advance your dream. Let it bring you a great sense of accomplishment that you are actively fulfilling your dream while enrolled at a community college.

However, there is much more to do in order to maximize your community college experience.

STEP ONE
REFLECTION QUESTIONS

1. What makes you unique?

2. What are your strongest likes?

3. What are your strongest dislikes?

4. What goals do you have for your life?

5. What can you do to push the boundaries of your life's dream?

6. How will/could your time at a community college be used to further the fulfillment of your life's dream?

STEP TWO
TIME MANAGEMENT

No doubt, you have heard of the importance of time management. Also, you most likely have had numerous opportunities in your lifetime to practice developing your time management skills. As you begin and progress through your academic career, these skills will become increasingly more important. This is especially true of community college students who typically have many responsibilities. For example, in 2007, seventy-seven percent of community college students were employed, with twenty-seven percent working full-time (AACC Research and Statistics). Consequently, an important part of succeeding in your community college experience is remembering to use good time management skills. While this may seem simplistic, many people who know the importance of time management do not use that knowledge to save themselves from wasting valuable time and energy. One of the greatest enemies of our dreams is mismanaged time; so, use the materials presented in this section to reinforce your intent to practice wise time management concepts.

The importance of time management will especially be felt as the number of responsibilities you face increases. While choosing to continue your education is one of the most important decisions you can make, it takes a considerable amount of time. Success will only come as you learn to manage educational, employment, familial, and other responsibilities. At first glance, this may seem overwhelming. In fact, there may even be times in which you are tempted to give up at various points in your academic career. Let me encourage you to use your time management skills to avoid some of those temptations and to help navigate your way through those that are unavoidable.

CHALLENGE PROCRASTINATION

One of the most important time management skills is to challenge any tendency you may have towards procrastination. The old adage the one should not put off until tomorrow what can be done today expresses an essential truth if you are to implement a wise management of time. While everyone struggles with procrastination at different levels and with different tasks, if your tendency to procrastinate is particularly acute, learning to challenge procrastination is especially important. Sometimes we procrastinate because we do not like the task or because we would rather spend our time doing other, more enjoyable tasks. At other times, we procrastinate because we feel that we can get by with a minimal amount of time and thought. Then, there also are those things that we put off because of some fear associated with the task before us.

Whatever the reason for procrastination, reaching your life's goal and your full potential will require challenging procrastination. Frequently, as one delays actions, the consequences of procrastination seem to grow more severe and more difficult to remedy. One of the best ways to challenge procrastination is to treat it with the disdain that it deserves. Convince yourself of the true negative consequences of procrastination and of your sincere desire to avoid those consequences at all cost, and you will be well on your way in overcoming this destructive habit. When it comes to procrastination, your attitude truly is a determining factor of how well you succeed. The next few guidelines are generally found to be powerful ways to win the struggle against procrastination.

PRIORITIZING RESPONSIBILITIES

First, it is important to learn how to prioritize. Since you may feel like you are being pulled in several different directions at once, due to your many responsibilities, you will need to determine the actual importance of each task you face. Doing this continuously is a key to true prioritization of tasks. For example, if you have a test in three weeks, studying for that test may not be as important as completing a paper that is due in a different class within a couple days. However, as the due date for the test approaches, it will become much more important to complete the studying process for the test. As you consider the different responsibilities that you are facing, a vital skill to develop is to learn how to prioritize the things that you need to accomplish and to determine in what order you will fulfill your responsibilities. However, do not make this process or prioritizing responsibilities an excuse for procrastinating. In other words, don't make the process of determining what you can put off a cheap excuse for not doing what needs to be done sooner than later.

DEVELOPING A SCHEDULE

Once you have learned to prioritize your responsibilities, it then becomes more important to learn how to develop a schedule. This schedule will be the primary tool used to accomplish as many tasks as possible as they appear on your priority list. However, for as many different personalities that exist concerning scheduling, there are an equal number of different methodologies for developing and managing schedules. Some prefer paper calendars, while others prefer one of the many electronic scheduling technologies now available. Each of these formats has its strengths and weaknesses. For example, paper calendars or to-do lists may be more comfortable for those who are less technologically inclined. However, many electronic devices offer powerful tools that can allow users to complete several scheduling tasks simultaneously. At the same time, electronic schedules are subject to the weaknesses of the technology and can be more easily accidentally deleted than paper copies.

Regardless of where you create your schedule, learning how to formulate a working to-do list is essential in successfully completing your tasks and reaching your goals. Once you have identified your most important priorities, then you must determine when you will begin the task and when it must be completed. This may vary as new or unexpected tasks arise and as due dates are changed. Also, there will be times in which your multitasking abilities will play an integral role in meeting deadlines. Be prepared to have times in which multiple projects are due at the same time. Developing the ability to work on more than one project at a time will both enhance and be enhanced by the development of a well planned schedule.

Overall, once you formulate your to-do list, it is imperative that you stick to it. It is at this stage that many are tempted by procrastination. Remind yourself how important it is for you to reach your ultimate goal. Keeping your attitude and attention focused on getting the most of your education will involve these and other good time management skills.

ALLOW TIME FOR REST

It may seem unnecessary, but as you develop your time management skills, it is important to also allow yourself to have fun and to rest. You remember what happened to Jack when he was all work and no play. It frequently is the case that as your responsibilities grow, your time for play and rest decreases. Strange as it may seem, some who have mastered prioritizing responsibilities and scheduling their time are the worst at failing to get enough rest and to have fun. The better you become at accomplishing your tasks, the more tempted you will be to only work and never play. More often than not, this is a mistake that will hinder your overall achievement of your life's goals. Without rest and engaging in responsible pleasurable activities, one is much more likely to reach burnout and to fail. Sometimes this may mean accepting a lower, yet still acceptable standard on some tasks. For example, a student who also has children may be willing to accept a slightly lower grade because (s)he spent much needed time with a child instead of reviewing for a test. There may be times when you may have to put off household chores in order to get out in the yard and enjoy working in a flower garden. Balancing work and pleasure sometimes involves making very difficult choices that only you can make. Remember to keep a high standard for yourself on your projects without compromising your health (i.e., rest) or those things that are important to you (i.e., family and social activities).

STEP TWO
REFLECTION QUESTIONS

1. List several of the responsibilities you are facing this week. Once listed, reorganize those responsibilities is order or importance.

2. How might this list be different in one week? How might their importance change after one month?

3. What are some specific steps you can take to allow for rest and personal interests while also meeting your responsibilities?

STEP THREE
CHOOSING A CAREER

F or many, academic pursuits at a community college are designed to prepare you for a career or to advance the profession in which you are currently employed. It may be a daunting task to consider a profession to which you would like to devote your life. For some, this is an easy task. You may have known for years what you wanted to do for the "rest of your life." However, sometimes we don't also know what profession we would like to choose, or we may have some apprehensiveness concerning future employment choices. Also, unexpected or unplanned career changes may bring you to a community college to acquire needed training. Wherever you are in the process of choosing a career path, there are a few guidelines that you can follow to maximize the benefits of the perfect occupational choice.

DETERMINE YOUR INTERESTS

A good place to begin your career choice process is through examining your talents and interests. As simple as it may seem, choosing a career in which you can use your unique talents and interests is vital. Sometimes people choose careers that are not tailored to their abilities, which can lead to burnout, job dissatisfaction, or even more serious problems. Since working in a career that makes you miserable is usually not an enjoyable prospect, now is a great time to give serious thought to what really makes you happy and what careers are the most appropriate for your talents. There are a number of tests that you can take to determine your personality type, which often can be used to identify general categories of professions for which you may be particularly suited. Most schools will have a counselor or student services department that can assist in using these resources to determine those professions most suited to your needs, desires, and personality.

At the same time, it is a valuable endeavor to not over rely upon standardized testing methods to determine what you would like to do in the future. While a guidance counselor can provide valuable insights, you should not let someone else pick your career for you. One method to utilize at this point could consist of simply writing down what things you enjoy and what types of activities fulfill your inner most desires. It may also be of value to write down those things that you know would not make you happy in a profession. For example, some people love to work with others, while some prefer to work in careers that allow them to work independently. Either way, once you have determined what skills, interests, and desires you wish to develop in a particular career choice, you can then search out those professions that make use of those aspects of your uniqueness. As with personality tests, your local guidance counselor or library should have resources that will help identify what careers utilize the skills and interests that you identified in your personal reflection.

While considering future employment choices, it is vital to also consider what your values are. As you reflect on your personal values, consider what you want to contribute to society and how you would like to do that. For some, making a contribution to medical research may be the best field in which they can express their values and skills. Others choose education, business, religious service, or other fields because they reflect the values that make them who they are. Regardless of which career field allows you to contribute in a way that best honors your value system, choosing a career that does not respect your values is an unwise endeavor. Few things are as fulfilling as contributing to a field that allows you to express your values; likewise, few things are as emotionally damaging as feeling stuck in a job that forces you to compromise your integrity.

INDIVIDUALIZED EXPECTATIONS

Once you have identified your unique talents and characteristics, there are a few additional concerns that can help you make the best career choice for your unique needs and interests. First, it is advisable to not make the bottom line the only factor you use in determining your career. While it may be that the anticipated salary level for a certain profession is of greatest importance, the prospect of working for a few decades in a profession that pays well but that brings you no satisfaction is generally not a practical expectation. While there have been some in our society's history who have amassed fortunes in careers that brought them no inward satisfaction, many have discovered that they would rather have served in a profession that paid less but that brought them a higher level of personal fulfillment.

Secondly, be flexible. Sometimes people choose a career and find happiness within that profession, only to discover a different line of work that could lead to even greater satisfaction. Considering both the rewards and the disadvantages of your prospective career choices is vital. Be willing to accept a future that may not be entirely spent in one field of employment. Also, experiment with the idea that you may prefer to give your time to a unique profession. There are many unique and interesting professions that can be both personally and financially rewarding without falling within any "top ten" categories. For example, a field that is currently being developed is the carbon management field. Degrees are being developed at colleges and businesses are pursuing management positions for those who enter this new field. As environmental health becomes an increasingly important international concern, this field likely will become an essential part of institutions of all kinds. While seemingly obscure, there are many options out there that may be new to your thinking but that could be perfect for your unique skills and values.

LIFETIME LEARNING

Learning never ends. To truly reach your life's goals, you will need a commitment to a lifetime of learning. Almost all professions evolve over time and require skills that may not have been required when one began his/her employment. Furthermore, life events and changes can create situations in which you may decide to enter a different profession altogether. Once you have chosen a specific career path, many professions will require continual training and education of their employees. Community colleges offer the types of courses that are often needed to develop the skills and knowledge base to either advance your current career path or to change career directions. Many times there also may be community education courses offered for a nominal fee that do not require a semester long commitment. Also, many community colleges are tapping into distance education options that allow students to learn from home, making it more manageable to attend credit classes while also managing family and work responsibilities.

Regardless of what option is the best for you to further your education and to learn needed skills, it is important that you to develop an acceptance of the value of being a lifelong learner engaged in continuous improvement. Accept the reality that your education does not end once you have obtained a degree. Many companies are investing time and money into furthering the education of their employees. Speak to a supervisor or human resources representative about the opportunities available in your organization for furthering your skills and knowledge base beyond the attainment of your degree. The bottom line is that learning really is a life long process, and those employees who avail themselves of learning opportunities are preparing themselves for a better and more secure future.

Step Three
Reflection Questions

1. What careers do you believe are best for you?

2. Why do you believe these careers are best for you?

3. What alternative career plans would you consider?

4. How best can you engage in a lifetime of learning?

Step Four
Social Networking

While enrolled in a degree program, it is important to involve yourself in social networking. Social networking may be defined in various ways, but for our purposes it is the process of developing contacts within your field of interest that can help you advance in your chosen career. This may consist of individuals who can serve as references or those that can help open a door of opportunity for you once you complete your education. Because you will eventually complete your coursework or degree program, making connections with other people will be vital to your long term success. This is especially valuable as you will compete for employment with other talented individuals who themselves have completed college degree programs. There are a number of ways you can accomplish this while also honoring your individual interests and goals.

Lasting Friendships

First, most educational institutions offer social activities on campus. Many of these social groups have no cost associated for student membership. Student government associations, religious student organizations, fraternities and sororities, and a host of other social groups often provide students a way to meet other individuals who share common interests and goals. These friendships often provide a source of joy and stability and can endure long after you have completed your education. Also, these social groups can offer leadership and volunteer opportunities that will help build your skills and résumé. These relationships may become extremely valuable in the future as you could use these contacts as references for employment opportunities. It is not uncommon for those who have involved themselves in social groups on campus to interview before an employer who was also a member of that same social group. As a consequence, making connections through the social activities on campus has the possibility of rewards in both the short and long term.

As you develop these social networks, it is also valuable that you make contacts both within the college environment and outside the walls of academia. In other words, while it is important to develop your social network with your peers on the college campus, it is also important to make contact with people who are currently in the profession in which you would like to work. Accomplishing this often requires getting off campus and doing some work in the community. This may be challenging if you do not intend to work in the community in which you are a student. However, it is advisable to still develop your social network as you never know when those contacts may provide benefits.

THE OUTSIDE WORLD

There are some specific steps you can take now, even if it is early in your academic career, which can pay huge dividends later. First, be willing to introduce yourself to potential employers. Doing this will help them associate a name with a face and will let them know that you are serious about your future profession. Secondly, look for any volunteering or assistantship opportunities. Coordinating your efforts with the resources in your college's student services department could be a better investment of your time than randomly visiting offices that may or may not offer such projects. Thirdly, if you work while enrolled in classes, look for employment opportunities that are in line with what you would like to do after completing your coursework. This will give you relevant experience that may more likely give you the skills and experience to get the type of job you are working towards.

ELECTRONIC SOCIAL NETWORKING

Increasing opportunities are available on the internet for creating a social network online. These resources, as with more traditional networking systems, provide both benefits and potential risks. For example, online social networking provides users the ability to meet with others is both formal and informal settings, using an easier and less time consuming format. Also, online social networking can allow you to meet people on a local, national, and international level, which can provide almost limitless networking opportunities. This can typically be done for free or for a nominal fee and can transpire with just a few strokes on a computer keyboard. However, internet hackers can break into computer databases that are used to store the information you provide social networking sites. For this reason, you should consider the risks and should never share information that could be used by internet hackers to access your personal records, especially in an era where cyber crime is on the rise (Wagner, 2007). Also, it is important to understand that future employers could use the internet to learn more about who you are and the benefits of possibly hiring you. This makes it vital that you carefully consider what personal information, both in text and pictures, you put online as anyone may have access to that information including future employers.

SELL YOURSELF

When you are in social networking situations, whether traditional or online, make it your aim to paint the best picture of yourself that you can. To do this, you should have a polished résumé. Regardless of how far you have advanced in your career, you should make sure that your résumé stresses the best qualities of who you are. This does not mean that you should lie or embellish the facts. However, while being honest, you should play to your strengths in your résumé. Also, be careful to follow best practices in résumé writing in relation to the format and the type of paper you use. There are a number of resources available at most bookstores and libraries that can guide you through this process.

Later we will deal with how to compose a résumé, but be mindful of the importance of being an advocate for yourself. Developing the ability to sell yourself to a potential employer by highlighting your strengths and experiences is very important in making needed contacts.

Step Four
Reflection Questions

1. Who in your present network could become valuable contacts in your future career?

2. What are some local areas into which you could tap for additional professional resources?

3. As you continue your academic career, what specific steps will you take to make important contacts to make your entry into the professional world the best it can be?

STEP FIVE
PROBLEM SOLVING

It most likely will not surprise you to know that life sometimes is problematic. Even the best made plans can sometimes be thrown off course. However, when problems arise, those who have a process for dealing with problems greatly increase their ability to overcome them. This is true of even more serious problems that one might encounter. While each problem may require a unique response, there are some general problem solving skills that can help in most situations.

IDENTIFY THE PROBLEM

To overcome problems you may face as you progress through your academic career, first you must clearly identify the source of the problem. As simple as this may seem, it sometimes can be challenging to identify the true cause of a conflict. At times, we try to treat symptoms and never get to the core of a problem, which fails to provide a remedy to the barriers that keep us from finding happiness and reaching success.

One important tool in identifying the problem is to ask WHY. It can be extremely helpful to actually write this down and to brainstorm about what is causing the problem you are facing. To discover why an event is happening, think about what specifically you are trying to solve. This can be challenging, because problem solving can sometimes be an emotionally charged process. It is in your own best interest to try to set aside more extreme emotional responses during

41

this process. As you brainstorm about the cause of why a dilemma is occurring, think about what could be the root cause. Consider what situations typically trigger the problem or what events usually occur before the issue arises. It may also be important to discuss problems with the people involved in problematic situations in order to truly understand why something is occurring.

For example, a possible issue that a college student might face is having difficulty turning assignments in on time. Having named the specific problem, the potential cause of the problem might be procrastination. It is especially helpful to remain open-minded in this process. To truly identify the source of the problem you may need to be open to accepting part of the responsibility for the problem. This is not always easy to accept, but having a willingness to accept personal responsibility (when appropriate) is important in solving problems.

IDENTIFY POSSIBLE SOLUTIONS

Having identified the issue that needs resolution and its cause, you are now ready to identify possible solutions. As with identifying the problem, this will require an open mind and the brainstorming of a list of possible options. Be willing to think creatively and to not necessarily limit yourself to the first solution that comes to mind. Also, it is important to keep in mind that this is not the time to choose which solution you will implement to solve the problem. Rather, at this point, you want to list as many options that you can possibly take to remedy the challenge you face. Be willing to accept options that may be either more creative or more traditional or even obvious. The important thing is to provide yourself several venues for creating positive change with any problem.

SELECT AN APPROACH

With your possible solutions in hand, now comes the task of selecting which solution you want to use to solve the problem. While some problems are more immediate and do not allow you to take a lot of time in contemplating solutions, if possible, allow yourself time to seriously reflect upon your options. At this point, you are ready to examine the solutions you listed earlier. It is valuable to consider both the potential positive and negative consequences of all possible options. Once this is done, compare your options. Some may have obvious flaws or negative consequences that you will want to avoid. However, there may be some problems that you face that could be solved in a variety of ways. During this phase of your problem solving plan, comparing your options can be difficult as more than one plan may seem reasonable. Fortunately, the implementation and verification phase will allow you to assess how well your plan of action worked and will provide you the opportunity to take a different route if the problem remains unsolved.

Having compared your options, consider what happened if you used any of these solutions to this or similar problems in the past. Taking these factors into consideration should help you narrow your choices. It is also important to not expect there to be a perfect solution. Sometimes you may have to make a compromise, though you should not risk your safety, integrity, values, or ambitions. The final phase of selecting a solution is to pick a solution that you believe will maximize your ability to solve the problem with the least cost.

IMPLEMENTATION AND VERIFICATION

The final phase of your problem solving solution is to implement your chosen solution followed by an examination of the effects of that solution. There will be times when you have followed a plan to potentially solve a problem only to discover that the solution did not positively affect the situation. For that reason, once you have implemented a solution, it is vital to verify whether that was an effective choice. If the problem was not remedied, simply go back to your list of possible solutions and select the next best solution. Continue this process until you have found the best situation possible. Setbacks may occur during the implementation of the solution you chose. However, it is important to neither give up nor to accept failure.

Having created your list of possible solutions should help create a more optimistic environment knowing that if one solution does not work you have more that could solve the problem.

Once you have completed this process, your skills in adjusting to and overcoming barriers to your educational goals will increase. For example, once a particular challenge has been successful met, you will then know one solution that helped in that specific situation in the past. As you grow, you will have tested solutions to various problems that can help expedite your efforts in similar situations in the future. In other words, as you successfully face problems, you will be able to build on past experiences and be able to face similar problems with greater ease as you progress towards the ultimate attainment of you life's goals.

Remember, everyone faces challenges and setbacks. Expect difficulties to be a part of meeting your goals. However, deciding to not let those challenges keep you from ultimately succeeding in your life goals is a major factor in whether or not you achieve those things that are most important to you. Sometimes this takes a great spirit of perseverance, but the end results far outweigh the discipline needed to succeed.

STEP FIVE
REFLECTION QUESTIONS

1. Make a list of how you will address problems in the future?

2. What are some current choices for which you could use a problem solving schematic?

3. What positive solutions in the past worked for you that you can use in the future?

4. How do you plan to better avoid repeating similar mistakes in problem solving situations?

STEP SIX
AVOIDING COMMON
PITFALLS

Every person is unique. While each person has their own interests, personality, and pleasures, there are a number of pitfalls that are common among many college students. Your success in your academic career is dependent upon successfully avoiding these pitfalls to the best of your ability. This does not necessarily mean that experiencing temporary setbacks in any one of these areas is uncommon. However, you should approach your academic career with the mindset of avoiding setbacks that have a permanent and negative impact upon your ability to reach your life's goals.

HEALTH CHOICES

Your first year in college is a time of great transition. For many, this is a first experience away from home for an extended period of time. For others, this is a test of their willpower as their time at college provides a taste of "freedom" from authority figures (i.e., parents, high school teachers, etc). Sometimes, it is at this point in the lives of many college students that poor health choices are made in regards to their diet and exercise (Payne, 2006). No doubt, you have heard of the "freshman fifteen" in which poor dietary choices lead to unintended weight gain. This problem is further augmented as students face great time constraints while balancing work, family, homework, and cocurricular responsibilities. Late night study sessions are often accompanied by pizza parties, sugary snacks, or other poor dietary choices. When this is combined with the possibility of decreased physical activity due to time constraints, students sometimes neglect to maintain their physical wellbeing. This problem may also be experienced with students who may not necessarily be overweight. Success in your academic pursuits should not come at the expense of your physical wellbeing. It is important that students have a keen awareness of any source of stress that may lead to unhealthy choices. This includes combating other eating disorders like anorexia and bulimia. Maintaining a properly balanced diet and engaging in even small amounts of exercise can provide great benefits to your wellbeing during your academic career.

In addition to maintaining a proper diet and exercise routine, your educational goals will more likely be met if you seek medical attention whenever necessary. This issue may seem simplistic, but there are times when college experiences may, unfortunately, necessitate medical attention. For example, staying up-to-date on needed vaccinations is vitally important as is taking preventative measures against sexually transmitted diseases. While social pressures and time constraints may create difficulty in making the best health choices, it is important for you to keep your mind's eye focused on the successful completion of your educational goals. Getting medical attention when needed and avoiding the neglect of any symptoms, even though seemingly minor, is essential in reaching your goals. Many colleges provide medical services for students or can refer students to local medical clinics that serve student populations. Often, these services are provided for free or for a reduced cost.

Each year, too many students waste precious time and talents because of substance abuses. Sadly, some not only loose their integrity and opportunity to reach their goals in life, but also may lose their life due to substance abuse. While social pressures to conform to certain standards may make it difficult to avoid tempting situations, it is important to remember that the cost of engaging in illegal drugs, alcohol, and the misuse of prescription drugs is detrimental to your self-worth and can permanently disrupt the attainment of your life goals. While research indicates that college life provides an environment in which an alarming number of students engage in experimentation with alcohol, binge drinking, illegal drugs, date-rape drugs, and other illegal or harmful substances should never be a part of your college career (*Gillespie, Holt, & Blackwell,* 2007). Avoiding situations that could lead to the use of such substances should be a priority in your attitude towards your academic pursuits.

EMOTIONAL WELLBEING

In addition to the attention your physical wellbeing requires, your emotional wellbeing is also a subject that is important in your academic pursuits. Sometimes the pressures that college students face can lead to depression or other situations that will require attention to the emotional aspect of college survival. Most colleges offer some type of counseling service that is often free and can be of great benefit whenever you feel in need of supporting your emotional wellbeing. This is often an invaluable service to students struggling with depression or other emotional issues. Similarly, students who practiced spiritual activities with great regularity before beginning their academic career sometimes fail to maintain those activities during their time at college. For those students, keeping a balanced approach to maintaining healthy spiritual activities can be of great benefit in their lives. Students can often find student associations or local churches that will help in providing opportunities to maintain their spiritual wellbeing.

TUTORING

Regardless of where you stand on the intelligence spectrum, there will most likely be times in which you struggle to pass certain subject areas, or to score as highly as you would like. Most two-year colleges provide tutoring services that are a wonderful resource. These are provided at no cost (in most cases) for students. You should not feel intimidated or ashamed to ask for help from tutoring staff. Many times the staff in tutoring centers are among the most caring and altruistic staff members one can find at a two-year college environment. Usually, these centers will provide assistance in mastering a certain subject, help in foreign language acquisition, or in proof reading papers. For all college students, this is one of the best services to utilize. In most cases, you can change tutors if you do not find success with a certain tutor, as each tutor with have his or her own teaching style and approach to tutoring.

DEVELOP A RÉSUMÉ

Since your goal is to eventually complete your academic pursuit, developing your résumé is an essential part of reaching success in your pursuits. It can be extremely difficult to try to compose a résumé from memory if you do not have a running record of your accomplishments. Whether you intend to transfer to a four year university or are looking to advance to your next job, having a well polished professional résumé is vital. In order to accomplish this, it is important that you continuously keep an updated listing of all your accomplishments. Keep a detailed list of those things that might possibly be useful on a résumé. When you actually submit a résumé, you may not list all of the achievements on your master list, especially since each résumé will be tailored for a specific opportunity. However, since many people are prone to forget some things over time, keeping a listing of all educational, experiential, and related accomplishments will help you be prepared to compose that perfect résumé when the time comes. Keeping this list stored electronically so that you can make updates regularly can be extremely helpful. Similarly, as you advance through the progression of your goals you have made important contacts that could be great potential references for future job application opportunities. This goes back to those social networking skill that are important in reaching your ultimate life goals. Remember to keep in touch with those important contacts, even after completing your degree program. You can also advance your career by gracefully leaving a current place of employment when you resign. As long as it is possible, try to not leave in such a way that it "burns bridges" or hurts your chances of using former employers as references.

Meeting Deadlines

One task that will be of vital importance in navigating your academic career is meeting important deadlines and remembering important dates. Ultimately, it is your responsibility to keep abreast of when paperwork for your particular institution or class projects are due. For example, many financial aid packages require the annual submission of forms that, if not turned in correctly or on time, could have a detrimentally negative impact on the progression of your coursework. Also, it is important to pay attention to the deadlines given in your course syllabi as your instructors may not always give reminders of when class projects are due. Be especially mindful of the courses that are required for your degree plan or certification. While you may have an advisor who guides you through course selection each term, it will be of great benefit for you to make sure you are taking the right classes. Similarly, if you plan on transferring to a four-year institution you should make sure that your coursework is transferable, especially in regards to the electives that you choose.

Utilize Library Resources

One of my biggest regrets about my academic career is that for the first few years of my academic career I did not avail myself to the important resources at my school's library. Now that I work as the director of an academic library, I understand more fully what I missed out on and the wonderful resources that could have made my first years a lot easier. While I may be biased because of my professional association within the academic library community, I believe that libraries are the center of academic learning. It has been my experience that students who regularly utilize the resources of the library are at the top of their class and perform better in their coursework. The value of your education and your ability to excel in your profession upon graduation can be greatly enhanced if you participate in what the local library has to offer.

At the present time, many libraries are adjusting to the ever evolving information age spawned by the internet. The consequence of this is that many community college libraries can now provide a wealth of resources that were unimaginable a few decades ago. When we think of libraries we often think of stacks of books. However, libraries now offer amazingly powerful resources for conducting research that are in electronic format. This means that in addition to the more traditional printed resources, libraries now offer electronic resources that may be overlooked during a casual walk through the library. Taking time to visit with a librarian about what types of services are offered at your school will be well worth the investment and can be of great benefit in making the best scores on your class assignments.

STEP SIX
REFLECTION QUESTIONS

1. What health choices are you making now that could negatively affect your physical wellbeing?

2. What health choices are you making now that could negatively affect your emotional wellbeing?

3. Schedule a time to take a tour of your library.

STEP SEVEN
POSITIVE
INTERPERSONAL SKILLS

There may have been times when you met someone that made a bad first impression as to the kind of person they are. Even though you may have had positive experiences with that person since then, you most likely remember that first encounter and use it in some way in evaluating them as a person, even if only on a subconscious level. This illustrates the importance of having good interpersonal skills and making a good first impression upon those you meet during your academic career. Your instructors, peers, potential employers, and others who have a powerful role in your life will often judge you based upon your interpersonal strengths and weaknesses.

COMMUNICATION SKILLS

Throughout your academic career, your communication skills will be tested through exchanges with instructors, staff, peers, and others. Having good communication skills will have a direct impact upon how successful these relationships are. One aspect of good communication is being a good listener. Keeping up with assignments and other responsibilities, learning class presentations, and other important processes in your educational pursuits will be measured by how well you listen. Your instructors will know how devoted you are to your class work by how engaged you seem during class. Attentively listening to class presentations will show your instructor that you are interested in the class and could influence the grade you receive. Their appreciation for your attentiveness could also help develop important relationships as you develop your résumé and make important social networking contacts.

While the field of communication studies can be rather complex at times, there are a few other practical rules to follow in order to make the most of your communication skills. First, it is important to remember names. While few people do not mind if you need to be reminded of their name once or twice soon after you first meet them, interpersonal relationships can be strengthened by learning and remembering names as quickly as possible. There are a number of techniques you can use to aid in remembering names. First, when someone tells you their name, use it in a sentence when you respond to their greeting. For example, if someone says, "I am Cynthia," you could respond by stating, "Cynthia, it is nice to meet you." By using the person's name in their presence, you are putting both their name and face into your long term memory. Furthermore, once you get to a place where you can make some notes, keep a written record of who you meet, who they are, their name, and their contact information if it is available. This is an easy way to refresh your memory and can spare you from embarrassing situations.

Furthermore, communication processes sometimes break down because the speaker does not carefully think through what they intend to say. Admittedly, there are occasions when you may not have the opportunity to think through what is said. However, anytime you make a presentation or plan on having an important conversation with someone, you should think through what you want to say by considering the best way to express your ideas. Doing this will help you avoid having to take back things that expressed unintended ideas. It can be beneficial to practice what you intend to say during important communication events. Having someone there who can provide feedback as to how you might improve your communication can provide important ways to advance the process.

ANGER MANAGEMENT SKILLS

Another important interpersonal skill is controlling possibly offensive emotions, like anger. Admittedly, anger is sometimes treated like the stepchild of emotions. Too many times we only think of anger as a negative emotion. On the contrary, anger can be a powerfully positive emotion. Throughout the ages, anger has led to the resolution of social problems, brought justice to cases of discrimination, and led many people to make personal improvements. At the same time, anger does seem to be a somewhat unique emotion in that, if left uncontrolled, it can lead to destructive ends. Sometimes mismanaged anger creates unimaginably harmful consequences. While this is true, anger plays different roles in the lives of various individuals. For example, one person may rarely struggle with anger issues; however, another person may struggle with anger daily. For this reason, each person should identify how anger affects them and the best way(s) to overcome negative anger. This is especially important when considering that we may live to regret actions taken or words spoken out of anger that cannot be undone.

One way to manage anger is to practice good problem solving skills. Having discussed guidelines for solving problems, it may be helpful to make sure you have developed a well planned methodology for dealing with problems as they arise. With your problem solving process formed habitually into the way you address situations, you will have a powerful ally in your approach to controlling anger.

Another invaluable tool in dealing with anger is through relaxation techniques. Many community colleges have counselors who can guide you through learning effective relaxation techniques. Also, there may be yoga or other similar courses offered that can provide valuable relaxation and meditation skills. One of the best places to learn relaxation methods is in beginning acting classes. These classes often offer students opportunities to learn inward reflection skills and ways to relax your physical and emotional stresses. Beginning acting classes also provide training for mastering emotions. Meditation, prayer, and other forms of relaxation can also be of benefit, especially if they are engaged in regularly. Oftentimes, when these skills are exercised during more peaceful times, they may kick in naturally when you are in a stressful situation and may not be thinking clearly.

It can also be helpful to examine the thought processes that you have during angry situations. Sometimes cognitive distortions, or illogical thought processes can create and/or feed our anger. Prejudices, biases, perfectionist thinking, jumping to conclusions, personalization, and other negative thinking can bring unwanted anger into our lives. By challenging any faulty reasoning in our thought processes and replacing them with better, more realistic ways of thinking we can solve some anger issues before they arise.

POSITIVE COLLABORATION

Nearly all academic activities require one to work effectively with others. Consequently, there are some additional generally accepted behaviors that can go a long way in building those needed interpersonal relationships. One of these is the ability to forgive. Undoubtedly, there will be times when people make mistakes that influence you. In some of these cases, you may either have to forgive the person or risk loosing a valuable relationship. This is especially true in those situations in which the one who did the damage is actively seeking your forgiveness. Hanging on to past mistakes generally only serves to make you bitter, unpleasant to others, and makes life extremely burdensome. Being willing to forgive those with whom we interact can not only ensure the survival of important relationships but can also make them stronger.

College environments typically are also very diverse. This means that you will have opportunities to interact with individuals from different cultures and with various backgrounds. It is a time in which you will cooperate with people who may not share the same worldview, religious views, political views, or aspirations to which you hold. To successfully navigate these situations, you need to be willing to accept personality differences and a global perspective that allows for the existence of multiple viewpoints. While you do not have to agree with the views of others, being able to coexist with others who do not share similar perspectives is an important part of healthy society that is too often lacking.

STEP SEVEN
REFLECTION QUESTIONS

1. What are some ways in which you could improve your communication skills?

2. What problems have you experienced due to poor communication?

3. How well do you practice forgiveness within interpersonal relationships? How can your improve in this area?

4. Do you have any prejudices towards other viewpoints?

CONCLUSION
THE ROAD AHEAD

Education is an extremely powerful tool. The education that you receive at a community college or other two-year institution of higher learning can help you attain your dreams and the self-efficacy needed to reach your goals. Having looked at some of the more important issues that you will face during your academic career, you are now better prepared for a bright future in which your highest goals are actualized. These tools should provide a foundation upon which you can more likely attain the biggest dreams you have for your life. Before you start on that journey, there are a few final considerations that can provide even more assistance to the attainment of your goals.

RESILIENCE

First, it is important that you not expect your college career to be like high school. Sometimes people who excelled in high school with little effort struggle in college because they expect to make the same type of grades with the same amount of work. Many times students receive greater leniency in high school than in a college environment. You should be prepared to take much more personal responsibility for fulfilling your responsibilities now that you have moved on to the next phase in reaching your life goals.

Secondly, have a positive attitude, even in difficult situations. This, at times, is easier said than done. Certainly, there will most likely be a few dreary and difficult days. You will face setbacks and challenges. Undoubtedly, you will make some mistakes. However, all of these are simply a part of the positive progression toward your ultimate goal of satisfying your life's dream. Looking at challenges from this perspective can make a world of difference. Also, unexpected challenges will come that you will be forced to face. These life occurrences, while sometimes difficult or discouraging, should be expected as challenges that everyone experiences. One of the best tools in your arsenal is you ability to rise above these situations through resilience. Determining to not simply become a part of a statistical group of people who give up when facing these challenges can be of great benefit in reaching your life's goals.

GIVING BACK

A final aspect of successfully navigating your academic career is giving back to those who have helped you to reach your goals. This includes giving of your time and, if possible, finances to perpetuate the future of the institution that provided the resources that made your education possible. This may also consist of participating in alumni activities and helping the next generation of students who attend that institution to succeed to the extent that you have. While you may not have enjoyed every class or teacher, the institution that made your education possible is striving to continue to serve the students that follow in your footsteps. Your involvement and support in the alumni affairs of your Alma Matter can help that institution make a better future for others who hunger for the attainment of their life's goals.

ADDITIONAL RESOURCES

A Compilation of Community Colleges by State by the University of Texas at Austin—http://www.utexas.edu/world/comcol/state/

American Association of Community Colleges—http://www.aacc.nche.edu/

Chronicle of Higher Education Community College News—http://chronicle.com/cc/

Clemson University's College Survival Skills—http://www.clemson.edu/collegeskills/

College Preparation—http://www.makingitcount.com/

Free Application for Federal Student Aid—http://www.fafsa.ed.gov/

Guide to Grammar and Writing—http://grammar.ccc.commnet.edu/grammar/

National Institute of Mental Health Information on Depression—http://www.nimh.nih.gov/health/topics/depression/index.shtml

Study Guides and Strategies—http://www.studygs.net/

Study Skills—http://www.how-to-study.com/

Taking Lecture and Class Notes by Dartmouth College—http://www.dartmouth.edu/~acskills/success/notes.html

U.S. Department of Education—http://www.ed.gov/index.jhtml

U.S. News & World Report College Rankings—http://colleges.usnews.rankingsandreviews.com/usnews/edu/college/rankings/rankindex_brief.php

BIBLIOGRAPHY

"AACC Research and Statistics". (2007). American Association of Community Colleges. Retrieved December 14, 2007, from <http://www2.aacc.nche.edu/research/index.htm>

Gillespie, W., Holt, J.L., Blackwell, R.L. (2007). *Measuring outcomes of alcohol, marijuana and cocaine use among college students: A preliminary test of the shortened inventory of problems—alcohol and drugs (SIP-AD). Journal of Drug Issues*, 37 (3), p. 549–567.

Payne, D. (2006). College quest to be thin includes unhealthy habits. *Medical Post*, 42 (20), p. 27.

Wagner, B. (2007). Electronic attackers. *National Defense*, 92 (647), p. 24-26.

NOTES